Mitchell

by Iain Gray

LangSyne
PUBLISHING
WRITING *to* REMEMBER

Lang**Syne**

PUBLISHING

WRITING *to* REMEMBER

79 Main Street, Newtongrange,
Midlothian EH22 4NA
Tel: 0131 344 0414   Fax: 0845 075 6085
E-mail: info@lang-syne.co.uk
www.langsyneshop.co.uk

Design by Dorothy Meikle
Printed by Printwell Ltd
© Lang Syne Publishers Ltd 2016

ISBN 978-1-85217-593-1

Mitchell

MOTTO:

By God's favour I conquer.

CREST:

Three ears of barley.

NAME variations include:

Michel

Michell

Michie

Mitchol

Mitcham

Mychell

Chapter one:

The origins of popular surnames

by George Forbes and Iain Gray

If you don't know where you came from, you won't know where you're going is a frequently quoted observation and one that has a particular resonance today when there has been a marked upsurge in interest in genealogy, with increasing numbers of people curious to trace their family roots.

Main sources for genealogical research include census returns and official records of births, marriages and deaths – and the key to unlocking the detail they contain is obviously a family surname, one that has been 'inherited' and passed from generation to generation.

No matter our station in life, we all have a surname – but it was not until about the middle of the fourteenth century that the practice of being identified by a particular surname became commonly established throughout the British Isles.

Previous to this, it was normal for a person to be identified through the use of only a forename.

But as population gradually increased and there were many more people with the same forename, surnames were adopted to distinguish one person, or community, from another.

Many common English surnames are patronymic in origin, meaning they stem from the forename of one's father – with 'Johnson,' for example, indicating 'son of John.'

It was the Normans, in the wake of their eleventh century conquest of Anglo-Saxon England, a pivotal moment in the nation's history, who first brought surnames into usage – although it was a gradual process.

For the Normans, these were names initially based on the title of their estates, local villages and chateaux in France to distinguish and identify these landholdings.

Such grand descriptions also helped enhance the prestige of these warlords and generally glorify their lofty positions high above the humble serfs slaving away below in the pecking order who had only single names, often with Biblical connotations as in Pierre and Jacques.

The only descriptive distinctions among the peasantry concerned their occupations, like 'Pierre the swineherd' or 'Jacques the ferryman.'

Roots of surnames that came into usage in England not only included Norman-French, but also Old French, Old Norse, Old English, Middle English, German, Latin, Greek, Hebrew and the Gaelic languages of the Celts.

The Normans themselves were originally Vikings, or 'Northmen', who raided, colonised and eventually settled down around the French coastline.

The had sailed up the Seine in their longboats in 900AD under their ferocious leader Rollo and ruled the roost in north eastern France before sailing over to conquer England in 1066 under Duke William of Normandy – better known to posterity as William the Conqueror, or King William I of England.

Granted lands in the newly-conquered England, some of their descendants later acquired territories in Wales, Scotland and Ireland – taking not only their own surnames, but also the practice of adopting a surname, with them.

But it was in England where Norman rule and custom first impacted, particularly in relation to the adoption of surnames.

This is reflected in the famous *Domesday Book*, a massive survey of much of England and Wales, ordered by William I, to determine who owned what, what it was worth and therefore how much they were liable to pay in taxes to the voracious Royal Exchequer.

Completed in 1086 and now held in the National Archives in Kew, London, 'Domesday' was an Old English word meaning 'Day of Judgement.'

This was because, in the words of one contemporary chronicler, "its decisions, like those of the Last Judgement, are unalterable."

It had been a requirement of all those English landholders – from the richest to the poorest – that they identify themselves for the purposes of the survey and for future reference by means of a surname.

This is why the *Domesday Book*, although written in Latin as was the practice for several centuries with both civic and ecclesiastical records, is an invaluable source for the early appearance of a wide range of English surnames.

Several of these names were coined in connection with occupations.

These include Baker and Smith, while Cooks, Chamberlains, Constables and Porters were to be found carrying out duties in large medieval households.

The church's influence can be found in names such as Bishop, Friar and Monk while the popular name of Bennett derives from the late fifth to mid-sixth century Saint Benedict, founder of the Benedictine order of monks.

The early medical profession is represented by Barber, while businessmen produced names that include Merchant and Sellers.

Down at the village watermill, the names that cropped up included Millar/Miller, Walker and Fuller, while other self-explanatory trades included Cooper, Tailor, Mason and Wright.

Even the scenery was utilised as in Moor, Hill, Wood and Forrest – while the hunt and the chase supplied names that include Hunter, Falconer, Fowler and Fox.

Colours are also a source of popular surnames, as in Black, Brown, Gray/Grey, Green and White, and would have denoted the colour of the clothing the person habitually wore or, apart from the obvious exception of 'Green', one's hair colouring or even complexion.

The surname Red developed into Reid, while

Blue was rare and no-one wanted to be associated with yellow.

Rather self-important individuals took surnames that include Goodman and Wiseman, while physical attributes crept into surnames such as Small and Little.

Many families proudly boast the heraldic device known as a Coat of Arms, as featured on our front cover.

The central motif of the Coat of Arms would originally have been what was borne on the shield of a warrior to distinguish himself from others on the battlefield.

Not featured on the Coat of Arms, but highlighted on page three, is the family motto and related crest – with the latter frequently different from the central motif.

Adding further variety to the rich cultural heritage that is represented by surnames is the appearance in recent times in lists of the 100 most common names found in England of ones that include Khan, Patel and Singh – names that have proud roots in the vast sub-continent of India.

Echoes of a far distant past can still be found in our surnames and they can be borne with pride in commemoration of our forebears.

Chapter two:

In the wake of conquest

Derived from the personal name 'Michael', or 'Michel', 'Mitchell' is of Biblical roots, stemming as it does from an ancient Hebrew term denoting 'who is like God.'

Alternatively, another derivation is from the Middle English 'mechel', 'michel' or 'muchel', denoting 'large', or 'big.'

Scots and Irish-Gaelic forms of the name include Macgille Michael, Uí Mhaoilmichael and Ó Maoil Mhichil, meaning 'patrons or devotees of St Michael the Archangel' or 'descendant of the devotee of St Michael' – but it was through the Norman-French form of 'Michel' that it became popularised as a surname in England.

This was in the wake of the Norman Conquest, a pivotal event in England's frequently turbulent history.

By 1066, Anglo-Saxon England had become a nation with several powerful competitors to the throne.

In what were extremely complex family, political and military machinations, the monarch was

Harold II, who had succeeded to the throne following the death of Edward the Confessor.

But his right to the throne was contested by two powerful competitors – his brother-in-law King Harold Hardrada of Norway, in alliance with Tostig, Harold II's brother, and Duke William II of Normandy.

In what has become known as The Year of Three Battles, Hardrada invaded England and gained victory over the English king on September 20 at the battle of Fulford, in Yorkshire.

Five days later, however, Harold II decisively defeated his brother-in-law and brother at the battle of Stamford Bridge.

But he had little time to celebrate his victory, having to immediately march south from Yorkshire to encounter a mighty invasion force, led by Duke William of Normandy that had landed at Hastings, in East Sussex.

Harold's battle-hardened but exhausted force of Anglo-Saxon soldiers confronted the Normans on October 14 in a battle subsequently depicted on the Bayeux tapestry – a 23ft. long strip of embroidered linen thought to have been commissioned eleven years after the event by the Norman Odo of Bayeux.

Harold drew up a strong defensive position, at the top of Senlac Hill, building a shield wall to repel Duke William's cavalry and infantry.

The Normans suffered heavy losses, but through a combination of the deadly skill of their archers and the ferocious determination of their cavalry they eventually won the day.

Anglo-Saxon morale had collapsed on the battlefield as word spread through the ranks that Harold had been killed.

Amidst the carnage of the battlefield, it was difficult to identify him – the last of the Anglo-Saxon kings.

Some sources assert William ordered his body to be thrown into the sea, while others state it was secretly buried at Waltham Abbey.

What is known with certainty, however, is that William in celebration of his great victory founded Battle Abbey, near the site of the battle, ordering that the altar be sited on the spot where Harold was believed to have fallen.

William was declared King of England on December 25, and the complete subjugation of his Anglo-Saxon subjects followed.

Those Normans who had fought on his

behalf were rewarded with the lands of Anglo-Saxons, and among them was a family of the 'Michel' or 'Mitchell' name who were granted lands in Surrey.

Within an astonishingly short space of time, Norman manners, customs and law were imposed on England – laying the basis for what subsequently became established 'English' custom and practice.

Bearers of the Mitchell name came to figure prominently in the historical record.

In the fourteenth century, Henry Mitchell was the judge recognised as the first holder of the title of Attorney General for Ireland.

Born in about 1320 at Killeek, in present-day Co. Dublin, he served in the powerful post of Attorney General from 1372 to 1373 and as Chief Baron of the Irish Exchequer from 1376 to 1377; he died in 1384.

From the fourteenth century to the nineteenth, one particularly intrepid bearer of the Mitchell name was Lieutenant Sir Thomas Mitchell, the surveyor and explorer responsible for the surveying and mapping of much of Australia.

Born in 1792 in Stirlingshire, and after a distinguished career with the British Army, it was in 1827 that he was appointed Assistant Surveyor

General of New South Wales and, a year later, as Surveyor General of the vast Australian continent.

It was a hazardous task, with some of his expeditions being attacked by the native Australians known as Aborigines as he and his party forged their way into the forbidding terrain.

In April of 1835, while trying to trace the course of the mighty Darling River, one of his party, the botanist Richard Cunningham, wandered off on his own in search of new flora and fauna.

When the other expedition members searched for him, all they found were fragments of his clothing. His body was never found, and it was believed he had been killed by Aborigines.

In an expedition the following year, Mitchell was able to confirm that the Darling River flowed into the Murray River, while he later also traced a route from present-day Sydney to the Gulf of Carpenteria.

He died in 1855, while the town of Mitchell and the Mitchell River, both in Queensland are named in his honour – while he also lends his name to the rodent-like animal known as Mitchell's Hopping Mouse.

Taking to the heavens, Maria Mitchell was the nineteenth century American astronomer who, by use of a telescope in 1847, discovered the comet later named in her honour as Miss Mitchell's Comet and also officially designated as C/1847 T. T.

Born in 1818 in Nantucket, Massachusetts and a distant relation of the eighteenth century American statesman and inventor Benjamin Franklin, it was through her father that she first developed her interest in exploring the heavens.

It was while working as a librarian in Nantucket that she discovered the comet.

This won her a prize that had been established some years previously by the keen amateur astronomer King Frederick VI of Denmark to discover a comet too faint to be seen with the naked eye and known as a 'telescopic comet'.

Her prize was a gold medal inscribed in Latin with *"Non Frustra Signorum Obitus Speculamur et Ortus"*, meaning *"Not in vain do we watch the setting and rising of the stars."*

Appointed the first female member of the American Academy of Arts and Sciences, in 1848, and two years later of the American Association for the Advancement of Science, she died in 1889.

The Maria Mitchell Observatory in her native Nantucket is named in her honour.

Chapter three:

Inventive minds

Bearers of the Mitchell name have also shown a particular flair for design.

Born in 1912 in Cleveland, Ohio, William L. "Bill" Mitchell was the American automobile designer who, through his work with General Motors (GM), was responsible for the design of an iconic range of cars that include the 1938 Cadillac Sixty Special, the 1949 Cadillac Coupe de Ville and some of the Chevrolet Camaro range.

Vice president of design for GM until his retirement in 1977, he died in 1988.

Going back to the nineteenth century, Dr Charles Mitchell, born in Aberdeen in 1820, was the Scottish engineer responsible for founding a number of shipyards on the Tyne after having worked as a ship designer for the firm of John Coutts in Newcastle upon Tyne before opening his own small shipbuilding yard.

This later merged with another yard to become the Armstrong Mitchell Yard; later known as the firm of Armstrong Whitworth, it is now part of BAE systems and Rolls Royce plc.

Also a philanthropist and the benefactor for structures that include the Church of St. George, in Newcastle, he died in 1895.

From automobiles and ships to aircraft, Reginald Joseph Mitchell, better known as R. J. Mitchell, was the British aeronautical engineer famed for his development of what became the Second World War fighter aircraft the Spitfire.

Born in 1895 in Kidsgrove, Staffordshire, and responsible for the design of many other aircraft, including flying boats and bombers, he died in 1937.

This was two years before the outbreak of the war in which his Spitfire played such a vital role in Britain's defence.

His son, Dr Gordon Mitchell, born in 1920 and who died in 2009, was the author of two books on his father – *R. J. Mitchell: Schooldays to Spitfire* and *R. J. Mitchell: World Famous Aircraft Designer*.

Also in the air, William Mitchell, better known as Billy Mitchell, was the U.S. Army general regarded as the 'father' of the U.S. Air Force.

It was after the end of the First World War that, as deputy director of what was then the U.S. Air Service, he vociferously and successfully campaigned for an increase in his nation's air power in event of a future war.

Born in 1879, he died three years before the outbreak of the Second World War, by which time American air power was already well on the way to become the formidable force it proved to be throughout the conflict.

The U.S. military aircraft the North American B-25 Mitchell was named in his honour.

Also on the field of battle, bearers of the Mitchell name have been recipients of the Victoria Cross (VC), the highest award for gallantry in the face of enemy action for British and Commonwealth forces.

Coulson Mitchell, born in Winnipeg in 1889, was a Canadian recipient of the honour during the First World War.

An engineering graduate, he enlisted in the Canadian Army in 1914 and was later posted to the Western Front. In 1917, he was awarded the Military Cross (MC) while serving as an officer with the 1st Tunnelling Company of the 4th Canadian Engineers.

The action for which he was awarded the VC occurred in October of 1918 at the Canal de L'Escaut, north-east of Cambrai, when he braved heavy enemy fire to disable demolition charges that had been set to destroy strategically important bridges over the canal.

He died in 1978, having served for a time on the staff of the Royal Canadian Engineers Training Centre at Petawawa, Ontario, and later during the Second World War as commander of the Royal School of Military Engineering in Chilliwack, British Columbia.

His VC is now on display in the museum of the Canadian Forces School of Military Engineering at Gagetown, New Brunswick.

Born in 1911, George Mitchell was a posthumous recipient of the VC for his actions during the Second World War.

He had been a private in The London Scottish (Gordon Highlanders) when, in January of 1944 during the battle of Monte Damiano, in the Italian Campaign, he braved intense enemy machine-gun fire to disable two machine-gun nests.

A German who had surrendered suddenly picked up an abandoned rifle and shot Private Mitchell through the head.

His VC is now held at the London Scottish Regimental Museum, London, while the citation reads: *"... His complete disregard of the enemy fire, the fearless way in which he continually exposed himself, and his refusal to accept defeat, so inspired his comrades, that together they succeeded in overcoming and utterly defeating an enemy superior in numbers and owning all the advantages of the ground."*

In the world of international diplomacy, George Mitchell is the American lawyer, businessman and politician best known for his crucial role in the Northern Ireland peace process.

Born in 1933 in Waterville, Maine, the son of a college janitor and a textile worker, he served for a time in the United States Army.

Receiving a law degree in 1961, he later turned to politics, serving as Democrat Senator for Maine from 1980 to 1995 and, from 1989 to 1995, as Senate Majority Leader.

Serving under President Bill Clinton as United States Special Envoy for Northern Ireland, he chaired the often tortuous peace negotiations that led in 1998 to the Belfast Peace Agreement, better known as the Good Friday Agreement from the day on which it was signed.

A recipient of both the Presidential Medal of Freedom and the Liberty Medal for his role in the peace process and also having served from 2009 to 2011 as United States Special Envoy for Middle East Peace, he has memorably stated:

"I believe there's no such thing as a conflict that can't be ended. They're created and sustained by human beings.

"No matter how ancient the conflict, no matter how hateful, no matter how hurtful, peace can prevail."

Nominated for the Nobel Peace Prize in 1998, he also served from 1999 to 2009 as Chancellor of Queen's University, Belfast.

As a businessman, he served from 2004 to 2007 as chairman of the Walt Disney Corporation while, as a lawyer, as chairman of international law firm DLA Piper.

Meanwhile one particularly infamous bearer of the otherwise proud name of Mitchell was the early twentieth century American serial killer Roy Mitchell.

It was in January of 1923 that the 31-year-old African-American was arrested for five separate murders in Waco, Texas, that included that of part-time deputy constable William Driskell by axing him to death in the garage of his own home and stealing some of his personal possessions.

The four other murders were those of 21-year-old Harvey Bolton, whose girlfriend he raped, Grady Skipworth, W.E. Halt and his girlfriend Ethel Denecamp.

In the hysteria of the time, 21-year-old Black-American Jesse Thomson had been wrongly identified as the murderer of Harvey Bolton. He was killed by a lynch mob and his body publicly burned.

Eventually tracked down and brought to justice, Mitchell was executed in July of 1923 in what was the last public execution in Texas, and the last by hanging in the state before the introduction of the electric chair.

Chapter four:

On the world stage

One of the most famous people of her generation and one whose memory is held in fond regard to this day, Helen "Nellie" Porter Mitchell was the Australian operatic soprano better known by her stage name of Nellie Melba and, later, as Dame Nellie Melba.

Born in 1861 in Richmond, Victoria, the eldest of seven children, her father was the noted builder **David Mitchell**, born in 1829 in Forfarshire, Scotland, and who immigrated to Australia when he was aged 23.

Married to Isabella Ann Mitchell (née Dow), he forged a highly successful career with major building projects that include the Scots' Church in Melbourne.

He died in 1916, by which time his daughter Nellie was firmly established as one of the world's leading operatic sopranos.

First singing in public when she was aged about six and later studying music in Melbourne, she went on to enjoy acclaim through performances at

Covent Garden, in London, in Paris and, in 1893, at the Metropolitan Theatre, New York.

Melbourne, meanwhile, had become her home city, and it is as a contraction or diminutive of 'Melbourne' that her stage name of 'Melba' derived.

In 1927 she became the first Australian to appear on the cover of *Time* magazine and, in the same year, was appointed a Dame Grand Cross of the Order of the British Empire after having previously been appointed a Dame Commander of the Order of the British Empire in recognition of her charity work during the First World War.

She died in 1931, and the many memorials to her include a statue at Waterfront City, in Melbourne Docklands – while she also lends her name to the dessert Peach Melba and to the crisp, dry toast known as Melba toast.

On a much different stage, and in contemporary times, Warren Misell is the veteran British actor better known as **Warren Mitchell**.

Born in 1926 in Stoke Newington, London, of Russian-Jewish descent, he is best known for his role from 1965 to 1975 of the bigoted London cockney Alf Garnett in the highly popular British comedy television series *Till Death Us Do Part*, written by Johnny Speight, and its sequels *Till Death* and *In Sickness and in Health*.

Voted TV Actor of the Year in 1965 for his portrayal of Alf Garnett, his many other awards include a 1976 *Evening Standard* Award for Best Comedy in London's West End for his one-man show *The Thoughts of Chairman Alf*.

Still on British shores, **Barbara Mitchell** was the actress best known for her roles in a number of television comedy series of the 1960s and 1970s that include *For the Love of Ada*, *Please Sir!* and also the children's programme *Lizzie Dripping*; born in 1929 in Richmond, London, she died in 1977.

A regular participant in popular British television panel shows that include *QI*, *Mock the Week* and *Have I Got News for You*, **David Mitchell** is the comedian and writer born in 1974 in Salisbury, Wiltshire.

It was while studying at Cambridge University and as a member of the famed Cambridge Footlights that he met fellow comedian and writer Robert Webb.

They subsequently formed the comedy duo of Mitchell and Webb, producing the television sketch shows *The Mitchell and Webb Situation* and *That Mitchell and Webb Look*.

Also on British television screens, **George Mitchell** was the Scottish musician renowned as having been the deviser of the highly popular late 1950s to 1970s show *The Black and White Minstrels*.

Born in Falkirk in 1917, *The Black and White Minstrels* evolved from his original radio programmes *The George Mitchell Choir* and *The George Mitchell Glee Club*.

The recipient of an OBE in 1975 for his services to musical entertainment, he died in 2002.

Back across the Atlantic from British shores, **Beverley Mitchell** is the actress and singer best known for her role of Lucy Camden-Kinkirk in the U.S. television series *7th Heaven*.

Born in 1981 in Arcadia, California, and with big screen credits that include the 1996 *The Crow: City of Angels* and the 2005 horror film *Saw 2*, her debut country music album, *Beverley Mitchell*, was released in 2006.

Known for his roles in the 1950s in television series that include the Westerns *The Adventures of Champion*, *The Range Rider* and *The Adventures of Kit Carson*, **Ewing Mitchell** was the American character actor born in 1910 in La Jolla, California.

Also known for his role from 1956 to 1959 of

Sheriff Mitch Hargrove in the television series *Sky King*, he died in 1988.

Yet another actor who found fame through his roles in a number of Westerns was **George Mitchell**, born in 1905 in Westchester County, New York.

With television credits that include *Tales of Wells Fargo*, *Gunsmoke*, *Laramie*, *Bonanza*, *Have Gun will Travel* and *The Virginian*, he died in 1972.

Still on a Western theme, Arthur Roy Mitchell, also known as **A.R. Mitchell** or Mitch Mitchell, was the artist and historian who, after working for a time as a ranch hand in New Mexico, became famous for his series of paintings of America's Southwest, including illustrations for Western-themed magazines.

Born in 1889 near the small township of Trinidad, in Colorado, his artistic work includes *Driving off Rustlers*, *Shadows at the Longhorn* and *Homeward Bound*.

He died in 1977, five years after being named an honorary member of Cowboy Artists of America. Much of his work is now on display in the A.R. Mitchell Museum of Western Art in Trinidad, Colorado.

Still in the world of artistic expression, **Charles Mitchell**, born in Newcastle in 1854 and who died in 1903, was the English painter of the Pre-Raphaelite period whose best known work includes his 1885 *Hypatia*.

Returning to the stage, **Chuck Mitchell**, born in 1927, was the American actor best known for his role of Porky in the 1982 cult comedy film *Porky's*; also with television credits that include *General Hospital* and *Bret Maverick*, he died in 1992.

Behind the camera lens, and renowned for what he termed 'giving a voice to the voiceless', **Denis Mitchell** was the British documentary-maker best known for his series of *People Talking* radio shows from 1953 to 1958 and the 1965 to 1967 television series *This England*.

Born in Cheshire in 1911, he died in 1990, the recipient of a number of awards that include, along with his collaborator Norman Swallow, a 1964 Grand Prix Italia Award for *A Wedding on a Saturday* – a television documentary of a northern English mining community.

Born in 1914 in Weyburn, Saskatchewan, William Ormond Mitchell was the Canadian broadcaster and writer better known as **W.O. Mitchell**.

Best known for his 1950's radio series *Jake and the Kid* and author of the 1947 novel *Who Has Seen the Wind*, portraying life on the Canadian Prairies, he died in 1998, the recipient of a number of awards and honours that include membership of the Order of Canada and being featured on a Canadian postage stamp.

Also in the world of the written word, Margaret Munnerlyn Mitchell was the American novelist and journalist better known as **Margaret Mitchell**, also known as Peggy Mitchell, famous as the author of the romantic novel *Gone with the Wind*, set during the American Civil War.

Born in 1900 in Atlanta, Georgia, and of wealthy Scots-American stock, she became a journalist, writing society columns for the *Atlanta Journal*.

She was a voracious reader and deeply interested in the Civil War period of 1861 to 1865, and it was after she was confined to home for a lengthy period after suffering an ankle injury that her husband, John Marsh, became rather exasperated with having to regularly fetch her books from their local library and bookstore. It is said that he exclaimed to her: "For God's sake, Peggy, can't you write a book instead of reading thousands of them?"

She carefully considered her husband's suggestion and he, to further encourage her, bought her what was then a state-of-the art Remington Portable No. 3 typewriter.

It was on this machine that she spent up to three years carefully constructing what became *Gone with the Wind*.

Throughout part of her writing process, that also involved deep research into the Civil War period, she would occasionally use pages of her rapidly burgeoning manuscript to help prop up a wobbly leg on her sofa.

Accepted by a publisher, apparently much to her surprise, it won the National Book Award for Most Distinguished Novel of 1936 and, a year later, the Pulitzer Prize for Fiction.

In 1939, it was memorably adapted for the film of the same name with Clarke Gable in the role of Rhett Butler and English actress Vivien Leigh in the role of Scarlett O'Hara.

Tragically, in August of 1949, Margaret Mitchell was killed after being struck by an automobile in her native Atlanta while en route with her husband to the cinema.

Born in 1901 and raised in Arbuthnott, in the

northeast of Scotland, James Leslie Mitchell was the journalist, short story writer and novelist better known by his pen-name of **Lewis Grassic Gibbon**.

Author of the celebrated *A Scots Quair* trilogy of novels, set in his native northeast and later adapted for television, he died aged only 34, while Arbuthnott is now host to the Lewis Grassic Gibbon Centre in honour of his memory.

In contemporary times, **David Mitchell**, born in Southport in 1969, is the English novelist whose best-selling works include his 2001 Booker Prize-listed *number9dream* and the 2004 *Cloud Atlas* – adapted for the film of the name in 2012 and starring Tom Hanks.

In the world of contemporary music, Roberta Joan Anderson is the multi-award winning Canadian musician, singer and songwriter better known as **Joni Mitchell**.

Born in 1943 in Fort Macleod, Alberta, of mixed Scottish, Irish and Norwegian descent, she rose from performing in small nightclubs to become an international recording star with hit albums that include her 1971 *Blue* – listed by *Time* magazine as among its All-Time 100 Albums.

The recipient of a star on Canada's Walk of

Fame, she also has the accolade of having been appointed a Companion of the Order of Canada and featuring on a 2007 Canadian postage stamp.

Born in 1947 in Ealing, London, **Mitch Mitchell** was the British drummer best known for having been a member of the band the Jimi Hendrix Experience; he died in 2008.

One bearer of the proud name of Mitchell with a rather unusual claim to culinary fame was the American food chemist **Dr William Mitchell**, born in 1911 in Raymond, Minnesota, and who died in 2004.

Employed between 1941 and 1976 with the General Foods Corporation, he was the inventor of a range of products that include quick-set Jell-O and powdered egg whites.

During the Second World War, he set his inventive mind towards producing a substitute for the dessert tapioca, because of a wartime shortage of the ingredient cassava.

His resultant tapioca substitute, issued as part of the field rations for U.S. infantrymen, was rather unflatteringly referred to by them as 'Mitchell's Mud.'